Alan's Little Book o̱f ...s

As a Motivational Speaker I have found myself reading dozens of books which contain inspirational thoughts and ideas. I guess such works will have influenced my own writings and, therefore, the occasional quips and provocations I offer.

In the Autumn of 2013 I was asked to present a series of school based assemblies, staff training events and workshops on the power of 'words' and so began 'Tweeting' through Twitter (#alanwords) some of the phrases I have used to make a point, provoke some thought or simply state what I believed.

This little book is the paperback version of those 'Tweets' and include many more talking points which I now offer for your consideration

Thank You for Your Interest...

Alan's Little Book

of

Thoughts, Provocations & Insights

ISBN
978-1-291-57968-0

© alan jones 2013

Life can get complicated all by itself and we can lose sight of what we once dreamed of being.

Keep it simple.

Focus on what matters now!

Find your own path and at every turn celebrate your seasonal, annual and life journey's

Don't tell anyone you care about them unless you can show them you do.

Simply telling them is about your need not theirs.

Do not make love a chore but make caring a habit.

Love needs to be nurtured not taken for granted

Love your friends, care for your acquaintances and show each their importance to you.

Yesterday is a memory, tomorrow is for dreamers, today is for being...

Learn from the past, create your future and act today.

For 'love' is

A home with many rooms...

A crystal with many facets...

A book with many chapters...

Sometimes things just creep up on you, all unexpected like ...

If I say "I love you" then I do and I will.

It requires nothing from you except to know that WE can choose how best to express it.

When you use the word 'love' do you do so to demand something, to control or appease someone?

Or do you really love them?

If you love and care for someone tell them today for tomorrow never comes and we may regret what we never said.

If you seek to know someone hear their words, read their writings, observe their actions and sit in their silence.

Know the difference between the words 'friend' and 'acquaintance'

Honour both and choose each wisely.

If we stand on the beaches of yesterday with the hopes of today maybe we can remember our dreams

The greatest demonstration of your love for another is to give them your undivided attention and unconditional love.

If you are my friend then listen to the spaces between my words, see the brightness in my eyes and sense the meaning in my heart.

Unconditional Love is the strength to let the person you felt the deepest connection with walk away – your sadness, a measure of your loss, set against the joy you are allowing them to seek.

If you love someone tell them how much...

If you are 'in love' with someone show them that you are...

In my mid 50's I think I am just about ready to grow-up a bit ...

Stay young at heart, be open to possibilities and play as often and for as long as you can...

Opening your heart is like bringing water to a desert.

Truth is about perception and what we believe shapes what we perceive.

The specific 'heaven' you 'go to' is built upon what you believe and the hell into which you can descend is based upon that which you can conceive.

That which you can conceive is not the limit of possibility

Of all the things you wear your expression is the most important

The Ego is you in relationship to yourself and the world

Egoism is your demanding the world to be in relationship with you

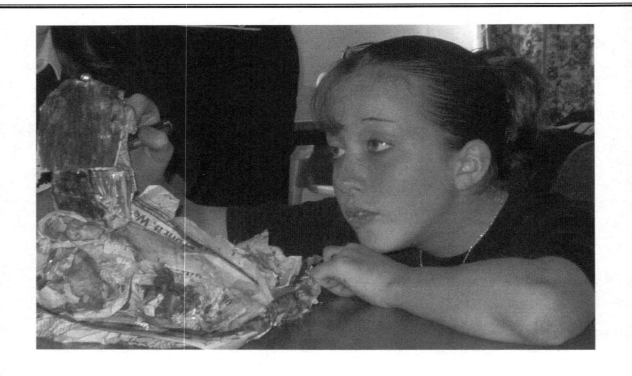

Seeing possibility in the things that others discard is the heart of creativity, the beginning of innovation

Love is not something to own or something you can tether.

It is a feeling, a freedom an acceptance which gives you wings

You can choose to consider each and every tear drop as water for the seeds of your future.

Love is more than a word, it is a set of harmonious behaviours which define how you love.

If you have fallen out of love with your lover remember that at one time, for one beautiful moment your words were your truth.

Are you spending time with someone because you think you should or because you believe it is expected?

Have you considered WHY?

There is a spark of genius in each and every one of us. Celebrate the spark within yourself

Love - a complex yet simple thing – perhaps love, like life, changes and within the differing textures and folds of loves caring cloak we find all the ways to express and to be love.

Perhaps falling out of love is a short had phrase for the transition between being IN love and loving to simply loving as in caring.

Those you have loved are with you, part of the tapestry of your life. Some of the tapestry threads are vibrant and part of the current picture; others are the weft and the weave which support the colourful stitches.

If you say you love someone tell them often, show them how much, hold the frequently and wrap your thoughts around them.

I've got 2697 Twitter followers; 1398 Facebook 'friends' yet I'm talking to myself and looking at stars alone!

Say's a lot ...

Welcome each and every sunrise for the number of our sunsets is limited

Magic is Real

It happens when you bring about change through the application of will and intention,

If your will and intention is in-line with your values and aspirations then that magic will be at its most powerful.

Without self awareness we can become the victims of spurious change rather than being the agents of that change.

All states of being – happiness, joy, harmony, loving relationships, peace – are journey's not destinations.

Your feelings are yours.

Others may try to toy with them, some may seek to manipulate them, YOU simply need to be honest with them.

You either 'do' or 'do not'.

It is generally the consequences of such 'no choice' situations which drive your action.

"I have to go to work, I have no choice", you will say.

Of course you do because you are choosing based upon the consequences of not going to work.

If you dream of feeling free ask yourself "what do I need to be or do in order to live that freedom?

The first thing you say to yourself in the morning shapes the rest of your day.

Some people spend most of their time saying what they are going to do rather than getting on and doing it.

Some people spend most of their time doing without thinking.

Consider the ancient dictum Know, Will, Dare, Keep Silent

KNOW
what needs to be done – plan

WILL
turn intention into action – do

DARE
act with belief and conviction – be

KEEP SILENT
speak through your deeds – become

*Words once spoken
cannot be unsaid*

*Words once heard
cannot be unheard*

*Words once understood
cannot be unknown*

Speaking your truth without seeking to be your truth is as empty as promises made out of desperation.

If you are willing to listen long enough even a rock will speak its truth

You are the Magic!

The Cosmos is not there to bend to your every whim and wish as some teachers proclaim

You can't order the cosmos but you can seek to understand its beauty, its' awesome magnificence and seek to find your magical place within it.

*The Cosmos doesn't speak English
or French or Zulu*

*The scientist seeks to learn about it
The mystic seeks to experience it
The poet tries to dream about it*

And Language serves to limit it

If we could recognize that the language we use serves as a label for experience then we'd see that every piece of religious text; every example spiritual writing and every dogmatic Cosmic Law are simply metaphors, allegories and projections of our limited understanding onto the unlimited, unknowable and infinite Universe.

The Spiritual Teacher...
   "I have made a connection"

The Scientist...
   "I am understanding the nature of that connection"

The New Age Space Cadet...
   "I have created an exclusive workshop based upon *my* interpretation of that connection"

The Mystic...
   "Wow, that was cool..."

If your relationship is your home then ensure that the building which houses it rests upon shared, firm foundations

There are different kinds of intimate relationships.

*There are
'healing relationships', 'transitional relationships', 'scripted relationships', 'survival relationships', 'convenience relationships', 'controlling relationships", 'transference relationships"...*

Each meets a need and a purpose – which type are you in and how would you like it to evolve?

Are you and your partner in the same relationship?

You are always making choices even when you think you have no choice.

You are unique – no one else has had the same experiences as you, learned the same lessons as you, loved, lost, cried and smiled in the same way as you.

Know this and celebrate the fact that you are someone special.

Maybe it is love's picture and focus which changes within the pages of the different chapters of life.

Friendship – a wonderful word defining the way we have agreed to love and support each other.

The mists of time may hide the reasons for things being as they are, but these things are part of your story, part of your history.

Do you need to know the reason you first loved in order to be that love?

Snowflakes will melt away in the morning sun

Snowballs turn into brown, muddy balls of mush

Your problems, when seen in isolation, can be seen as snowflakes so why lump them together to make something more permanent than it needs to be?

If all you do is moan and complain about your lovers shortcomings to others, why are you still with them?

Treat your words as seeds with meanings that grow in the hearts and minds of others.

If you say you love me then promise me nothing but be the hand that I can hold, the ears that will listen and the friend who will not judge.

Four words to change the world

Tell Me Your Story

One Action to make change continual

Listen

It's OK to let the journeys of others become the landmarks on your road, but that does not mean you have to follow in their footsteps.

Create, live and be your own journey.

Loneliness is not a state of being it is a state of mind

I love you because of who you are not because of what I want you to be

There is a difference between ego and egotism

Love - the force which keeps us in a continual, creative and caring orbit around each other.

Words are anchors for experience.

*Use them wisely to create
meaningful moments
with each other.*

There is an end to every journey and perhaps what matters most is not how far you travelled, but who and what you touched along the way.

Remember for the individual perception is truth…

Shared truths only come from seeking to learn from each other

The job of any parent, teacher, therapist or guru is to make themselves redundant.

When the child can decide for their-self, the student can direct their own learning, the client can be empowered and the seeker is on their path then each may retire.

True learning comes from the sharing the truths of others and bathing in the light of their experience.

Your experience is yours and yours alone; it was created by your interaction with the world.

It is an honour to be invited into another's world and share their truths.

There is no need to challenge their interpretations of their own experiences unless invited.

If, however, they insist that their interpretations are a universal truth outside of themselves then it is right and proper that you find the way to question, probe, explore and learn.

*Attention flows
where emotion goes*

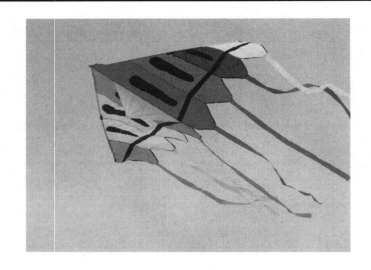

I love you so please ...

Teach me to be the wind which gives you flight

No person, no religion, no cult, no faction, no group has the monopoly on truth.

Wealth is a matter of perception

Richness a matter of action

Contentment a matter of connection.

Something once learned can never be unlearned

What is possible is a matter of perspective and belief

What is impossible is a matter of belief and perspective

Negativity is like a virus

It spreads and it multiplies

It feeds on optimism and creativity

It excretes stagnation and dullness

It alters the way you think

It defines the way you act

Love is like the roots from which trees to grow. The deeper the roots the more sturdy the tree...

Why make icy, hard snowballs out of delicate, gentle snowflakes?

Some people do not know the difference between skepticism and cynicism; between pragmatism and negativity; between improbable and impossible.

For them everything is viewed through the tunnel vision of the doubter rather than the peripheral vision of dreamer.
So whilst the dreamer may trip over rainbows the doubter will never really see the sun.

Just for today I am going to go out of my way to see what is good in this world; to talk about my dreams and recognize the inspirational.

And you never know if I like it I may do the same tomorrow.

Of course you don't simply ignore the problems, challenges and upsets in your life.

That would be superficial and flippant. Worries, concerns, fears, loss and hurt are all part of your life.

However if you allow them to swamp you, to consume you, they become your life.

*Your life has many truths
find a balance between them*

An empty bench is simply waiting for the right person to come and share the moment.

Science speaks of energy and power in very specific ways – it's all about 'the ability to do work'; the potential to overcome inertia.

It can be measured directly by science.

Love, as the mystics know, gives humans the ability to create change and inspires the work which brings that change about.

It cannot be measured directly by science.

Neither Mystic nor Scientist would doubt the reality of the others descriptions and indeed it is only the ignorant who fail to recognize the value and relevance of each approach to knowing; the different ways of describing.

"Feelings", someone said, "are the sensory symptoms of thought patterns created by interaction with the environment".

Well that's what they are neurologically, but it is our feelings (or their neurological correlates) that motivate behaviour.

So love, the neuro-chemical excitement involving oxytocin related endorphins and similar neurotransmitters, may be the result of evolutionary, environmental and biological drives – but how we express it behaviourally and culturally is a much deeper, complex and poetical thing.

The path to personal enlightenment and knowledge begins with one question...

How do you Know What You Know?

You may not always live up to your expectations of yourself and that's OK.

You can choose to forgive yourself and try again...

Treat others as you would like to be treated and do not expect them to understand that and return your attention – simply recognize that you are living your truth as fully as you can.

Find the time to BE present in the NOW and allow the moment to absorb and enliven every sense.
**Focus on BE-ing
rather the BE-coming**

If your lover is your friend then no topic is off limits; no fear to great to be eased; no desire to passionate to be expressed.

In relationships you need to feel free to relate your thoughts, feelings, dreams, desires.

Love Making with your partner is something that happens during every moment of your being together.

It is the conversation, the gentle touches, the hugs, the moments of silence and the desire to express the love you feel.

Making Love is the intimate, physical exploration of the love you share.

How will you know when you are happy?

Happiness, the thing to which many aspire, needs to be defined in terms of the things which bring happiness; the behaviours which surround it and the things it allows you to do.

Some folks create an idealized, abstracted 'destination' called happiness without thinking about the What, Who, Where, When and How of being happy.

Without knowing what makes you happy you'll never reach the destination and probably not enjoy the journey.

Love can be the desire which feeds your dreams; your dreams of love can inspire your actions and your actions can define your path.

That doesn't mean you will find love, but you will be better placed to recognize it when it is given to you.

You have to sit with knowledge and integrate experience in order to become wise.

Wisdom is earned not learned.

Every loss can break a heart but consider that that pain is for what was and not what is.

Hold onto the best of what was; resolve the pain of what is and slowly allow your-self to step into a future of what is yet to come without prejudice, fear or despair.

You can't demand to be loved it is a gift freely given, a dream which can be shared and a moment sometimes missed.

Believe in the Magic of Your Dreams for within each lies the expression of your desires; the seeds of possibility and the motivation to take action.

You cannot fail!

You merely discover what will or won't work

Let's face it, you didn't learn to walk by simply standing up...

NO! You learned to walk by falling over; each step encouraged by those who cared, each tumble eased by a loving touch.

In order to succeed find the care, support and love of others and be prepared to fall over!

If trees compete for the same piece of sky and the same piece of earth they will wither in each other's shadow

Control is largely an illusion.

It is the idea of a temporary ownership of power which changes as soon as new information or experiences are fully understood.

If you feel controlled you either lack the information, experience or emotional strength to counter the controlling influence – find that friendly support.

If you feel 'in control' then you don't fully comprehend the instability of your position – look to your own insecurities.

There are four key skill areas which we need to develop as individuals...

The ability to access and assess information

The ability to communicate in a wide variety of ways

The ability to lead and manage self

The ability to manage change

Money can buy company but only friends earn friends.

Thank You for choosing to be here, with me on this journey at this point on the road.

And if tomorrow our paths take different routes to different people and different places know that I will cherish this moment and honour all that we have shared.

Was there a time when I did not know that before you came you were ready to go?

Life does not consist of black and white or good and evil but as wonderful shades of grey against which starlight sparkles and love can shine.

Love, a momentary lapse of sanity wherein all that we feel is focused on a singular desire to be with...

Sanity, a moment of clarity wherein all that we know is fused with purpose to dream with ...

Insanity, a momentary fear that there is no love to counter the sense of being alone with ...

$$S = PMA + A$$

Success is the product of positive mental attitude plus application!

*The next time you find yourself saying **"I Can't"** try saying **"I Won't"** to see if that is what you really mean*

Anger demands the target of that anger to show guilt

AND

Guilt invites the target of that guilt to show anger

There can be no rights without responsibilities.

It's a shame that far too many argue for what is theirs whilst trampling on that which is rightfully others.

*Focus, balance, poise and beauty
belong to those who work to know
themselves and are willing to say*

'Here I Am – Accept Me for being Me'

Seek the next vibrational level of incarnate reality whilst dancing to stolen tribal chants and invoking the indigo ray of the violet flame of some unnamed ascended master if you so wish...

Or

Be in the rain, splash in the mud and make love under the stars...

*And **then** tell me which was the most spiritual!*

Levels of Reality

Scientific Reality
    Everything is Objective
    Observable, Measureable, Testable, Theories are Tentative

Psychic Reality
    Everything is Subjective, Interpretation, Personal Resonance, 'Truth'

Shamanic Reality
    Everything is Symbolic, Metaphor, Allegory, Signs, Portents, Omens

Mystical Reality
    Everything is Everything
    Relax – Don't Worry Be Happy

Psychic from the Greek meaning mind

YOU
EYES
EARS
HEART
UNDIVIDED
ATTENTION

The Chinese pictogram for the word LISTEN defines the nature of true listening

Intuition is the sum total of the sensory experience, memories, associations, emotions and situations which are processed by your unconscious and presented as some kind of 'knowing' or 'sense' to your conscious mind.

There can be a trans-personal, mystical and spiritual side to our intuition where what is known is something apparently beyond the self.

If you ask me to lie for you today and I do can you promise me you will never doubt my truth tomorrow?

Sometimes wisdom stands alone and silent amid the noise generated by those with knowledge

Consider, there may be no single love of your life, no single soul mate, but simply the truth that each and every love 'was' and 'will ever be' the true love, the soul mate, for that chapter, that page or that sentence in the book of your life.

Let me be the sun to your moon; the winter to your summer and the reason in your life for as long as love shall last.

Hope alone is merely the 'salve', the ointment we use to make us feel better when things are at their darkest.

But when Hope and Will combine there is the potential for great change.

The Magician

is

The Trickster in the Spring
The Wizard in the Summer
The Oracle in the Autumn
The Sage in the Winter

The Magician Provokes Change

Be the Magician in Your Own Life

A space of loneliness is not the same as an empty place

Remember you and I are on our own journey and if, for now we can share the road then let us do so joyfully and through choice.

There is a truth in simplicity and a purity in innocence but is it too often the case that we mistake simplicity for simple and ignorance for innocent?

When my love holds you in these clumsy arms feel the strength I offer...

When my love caresses you with these calloused hands feel the support I wish to give...

When my love touches you with these fevered lips feel the words I wish to utter...

It has been said that to everything there is a season, and that applies to every facet of you, your life and your relationships.

Enjoy the stirrings of spring, the heat of summer, the cool of autumn and the solace of winter which can exist in every moment when you choose to reflect upon your life and love.

If your smile is not understood use your actions to explain.

If your actions do not speak then use words.

The moment you stop communicating in any relationship is the moment that it begins to wither.

Don't let the labels others use to describe you limit or define your journey

Words which are expressions of thoughts and feelings should inspire action if their truth is to be expressed.

Beware of the gulf between saying and doing!

*What you call God,
I may call Love*

*What you call Angel,
I may call Friend*

*What you call Faith,
I may call Knowing*

Knowing is not knowledge, it is a deep wisdom born of experience, intuition and a sense of this is where I need to be, what I need to be doing at this moment in this life – and trusting that all be will OK.

It is **faith in a real sense**, but whereas faith can be blind, like justice, and passive as in fatalistic, knowing is acting upon what you trust.

Wars are created in fear, born in ignorance and maintained through prejudice.

Blind faith in the reason for war rather than the 'knowing' of its causes is the armor of the warrior.

Words and the exploration of truths through conversation are the tools of the peacemaker.

Have you ever noticed that many wars include the burning of the books of the vanquished?

This destruction of the writings of a foe are attempts to quiet the words of the victims and silence the thoughts they sought to share.

Your Mission Should You Want To Accept It

Help others; share the sun and the moon if you so choose and have fun along the way...